SCIENCE
PROJECTS

LIGHT

Trevor Day
Photography by
Chris Fairclough

WAYLAND

Produced for Wayland Publishers Ltd by
The Creative Publishing Company
Unit 3, 37 Watling Street, Leintwardine
Shropshire SY7 0LW, England

First published in 1997 by
Wayland Publishers Ltd,
61 Western Road, Hove,
East Sussex BN3 1JD, England

British Library Cataloguing in Publication Data
Day, Trevor. 1955-
    Light (Science Projects)
    1. Light – Juvenile literature 2. Light –
    Experiments – Juvenile literature
    I. Title
    535

ISBN 0 7502 2046 5

Printed and bound in Italy by
G. Canale & C.S.p.A., Turin

Designers: Ian Winton and Heather Blackham
Editors: Paul Humphrey and Tamsin Osler
Consultant: Jeremy Bloomfield
Illustrations: Julian Baker
Commissioned photography: Chris Fairclough

Picture acknowledgements
The publishers would like to thank the following
for permission to reproduce their pictures
Bruce Coleman: pages 4, 10 (Harald Lange), 20
(John Shaw); **NASA** page 4; **Oxford Scientific
Films:** page 28 (Javed Jafferji); **Science Photo
Library:** pages 14 (Bill Longcore), 32 (Harold
Edgerton), 41 (Gordon Garradd), 42 top (Dr Jeremy
Burgess), 42 bottom (Andrew McClenaghan), 44
(Françoise Sauze), cover (Mehau Kulyk); **Tony
Stone Images**: pages 6 (David Muench), 8 (Glen
Allison), 23 (Jeremy Horner), 38 (Tim Davis).

The publishers would like to thank the staff and
pupils of The Drove Junior School, Swindon, for
their help in the preparation of this book. The
publishers also wish to thank Philip Harris
Education for kindly loaning various materials used
in the projects in this volume.

NATIONAL CURRICULUM NOTES

The investigations in this book are cross-referenced to Programmes of Study for Science at Key Stages 2, 3 and 4.

SUNLIGHT Demonstrates how the rotation of the Earth causes the movement of the Sun across the sky. KS3 Sc4, 4a, 4b & 4d

SOURCES OF LIGHT Making a controllable light source for use in experiments. KS2 Sc4, 3a; KS3 Sc4, 3a

TRAVELLING LIGHT Light travels very fast and in a straight line. KS2 Sc4, 3a; KS3 Sc4, 3a & 3c

LETTING LIGHT IN Transparent, translucent and opaque materials. How shadows are formed. KS2 Sc4, 3b; KS3 Sc4, 3b

ME AND MY SHADOW How shadows behave. Creating a shadow play. KS2 Sc4, 3b; KS3 Sc4, 3b

HOW WE SEE THINGS Reflected light from objects enters our eyes. KS2 Sc4, 3d; KS3 Sc4, 3d

ON REFLECTION How light is reflected from objects. KS2 Sc4, 3c; KS3 Sc4, 3e

MORE REFLECTIONS and **MIRROR, MIRROR...** How light is reflected at plane surfaces. KS2 Sc4, 3c; KS3 Sc4, 3e

MIRROR IMAGES How light is reflected at plane and curved surfaces. KS3 Sc4, 3e

UP PERISCOPE! and **KALEIDOSCOPES** Modelling projects that show useful ways of reflecting light off plane mirrors. KS3 Sc4, 3e

BENDING LIGHT and **BENDING MORE LIGHT** How light is refracted at the boundary between two different materials. KS3 Sc4, 3f

TAKING A SNAPSHOT How light behaves in a simple camera. KS2 Sc4 3a; KS3 Sc4, 3a

LENSES, IN FOCUS and **SEEING DOUBLE** How our eyes detect and focus the light reflected from objects. KS3 Sc4, 3d; KS4 Sc2, 2f (single science), 2j (double science)

MAKING RAINBOWS White light can be dispersed to give a range of colours. KS3 Sc4, 3g

SUBTRACTING COLOURS and **ADDING COLOURS** The effect of colour filters on white light. How coloured objects appear in white light and in other colours of light. KS3 Sc4, 3h & 3i

CONTENTS

SUNLIGHT

Light affects almost everything we do. Without light from the Sun there would be no life on Earth. The planet would be cold and lifeless. The presence and absence of natural light – daytime and night-time – governs when we choose to be awake and when we choose to sleep. If we want to continue work during night-time then we must rely on various sources of artificial light, like electric lights.

This photograph, taken from space, shows one half of the Earth completely in daylight.

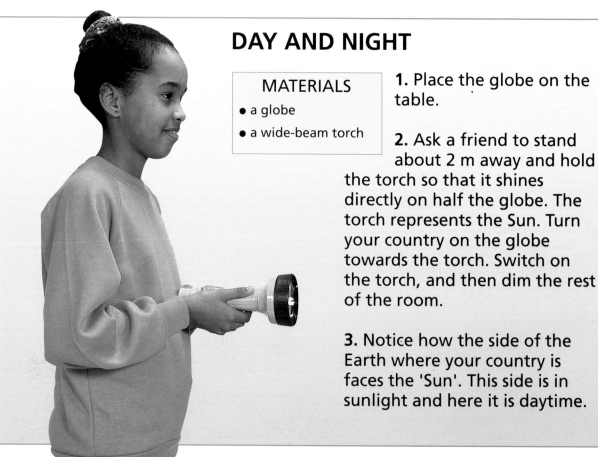

DAY AND NIGHT

MATERIALS
- a globe
- a wide-beam torch

1. Place the globe on the table.

2. Ask a friend to stand about 2 m away and hold the torch so that it shines directly on half the globe. The torch represents the Sun. Turn your country on the globe towards the torch. Switch on the torch, and then dim the rest of the room.

3. Notice how the side of the Earth where your country is faces the 'Sun'. This side is in sunlight and here it is daytime.

The Earth spins on its axis once every twenty-four hours. During part of that twenty-four-hour period the place you live on the Earth is turned towards the Sun and is bathed in sunlight. It is daytime. During the other part of the twenty-four-hour period the place you live is turned away from the Sun and is in shadow. It is night-time. The experiment below shows how the Sun creates daytime and night-time.

This photograph shows half of the Earth in daylight. The other half is in shadow and there it is night-time.

4. Looking from above, turn the globe anti-clockwise slowly. This shows how the Earth turns in space.

5. When you have made a half turn of the globe, you will notice that your country is now directed away from the 'Sun' and is in shadow. Now it is night-time.

6. Keep turning the globe. Notice how the 'Sun' lights up the Earth from east to west. So Britain is in daylight before North America. The Sun rises five hours earlier in London than it does in New York. This is why there are different time zones around the world.

5

SOURCES OF LIGHT

Very hot objects produce light. The Sun – at 15 million °C – provides most of the natural light on Earth, but there are other natural sources. Lightning, the sudden release of massive amounts of electrical energy, creates huge amounts of light. And burning objects – such as dry wood struck by lightning – produce a yellowy light. However, things do not have to be hot to generate light. Some animals produce their own light. Fireflies (also called glow-worms) flash a green light from their rear end to attract a mate. They do this using a natural chemical reaction – no heat is involved.

To help us see in poor light conditions we have developed many artificial sources of light. In prehistoric times the first artificial sources were probably campfires. Since then, humans have harnessed fire as a source of light in candles, oil lamps and gas lamps. Within the last hundred years or so, electricity has become our main source of artificial light. We take for granted the electric bulbs and fluorescent tubes we switch on every day.

The Sun is the main source of natural light on Earth. You can see shafts of sunlight in this photograph.

MAKING A RAYBOX

1. Glue the block of wood to the base at one end of the shoebox.

2. Paint the inside of the shoebox, the lid, the piece of card and the wooden block black.

3. Tape the torch to the wooden block so that the torch's beam strikes the middle of the opposite end of the box. Cut five 2 cm x 2 mm vertical slits in this end of the box, the first in the centre and the others spaced 2 mm apart on either side.

4. In the centre of the piece of card cut another slit 2 cm x 2 mm.

5. Switch on the torch and darken the room. You will see five beams of light emerging from the raybox. Now clip the card with one slit inside the end of the box so that the slit overlaps with the middle slit in the box. Now a single beam of light will emerge. You will use both these effects in the experiments in this book.

Why was it necessary to paint the inside of the raybox black?

MATERIALS

- a shoebox and lid
- a piece of card the same size as the end of the shoebox
- 2 paper clips
- matt black poster paint
- a paintbrush
- a small, powerful, narrow beam torch
- a block of wood about 10 cm long, 4 cm wide and 2 cm deep
- strong glue
- dark sticky tape
- a modelling knife
- a cutting board
- a metal straight edge

WARNING!

- Do not point the torch directly into anyone's eyes.
- Take care using the knife and cutting board.

TRAVELLING LIGHT

Light travels very fast indeed, much faster than sound. That is why you can see a flash of lightning before you hear the thunderclap that it creates. Sound covers just 340 m in every second. Light, on the other hand, travels at 300,000,000 m per second!

Under normal conditions, light travels in straight lines. You cannot usually see a beam of light from a torch, but you can see a small, bright spot when the beam hits something, like a wall.

This experiment shows how light travels.

You can see lightning before you hear the thunderclap because light travels faster than sound.

STRAIGHT TO THE POINT

MATERIALS
- a raybox and card with one slit
- a hole punch
- three squares of dark card
- modelling clay
- a straight knitting needle
- a sheet of white card
- a joss stick
- safety matches

1. Set up the raybox.

2. Punch holes in the three cards at the same height as the beam from the raybox. Mount the cards in an upright position on a table using small pieces of the modelling clay.

3. Position the cards so that their holes are in a straight line. Check this by passing a straight knitting needle through the holes. Position the white card at the end of the row of cards.

WARNING!
- Take care using the joss stick and matches.

4. Darken the room. Shine the light beam through the holes. You should find a ray of light passing through the holes and forming a small bright spot on the card.

5. Move the second card about 2 cm to one side. Now what can you see on the white card? Where does the ray of light fall? What does this tell you about whether or not a light ray bends?

When a ray of light travels through the air you cannot see it. You only see the presence of light when it strikes something – like the paper or the card. You can show rays of light travelling through the air using small particles such as smoke particles. Light the tip of a joss stick, blow out the flame, and darken the room. Gently blow the smoke into the beam from the raybox. What do you see? Blow smoke into the ray of light passing through the cards. What do you see? What does this tell you about the way light travels?

Did you know?

The distances in space are so enormous that we use light – the fastest thing we know – as a means of measuring them. The measurement is the light year – the distance that light travels in one year (nearly a thousand billion kilometres). The most distant objects we know are more than 13 billion light years away!

LETTING LIGHT IN

Everyday things respond to light in different ways. The passage of light through an object is called transmission. Some objects transmit light more readily than others.

Transparent materials allow all or nearly all light to pass through them. Such materials include clean air, clean water and clear glass. We can see through them and the image we see is very similar to the original object. Other materials are translucent. They allow some light through, but some of the light is scattered in all directions by particles within the material.

You can sometimes see through such materials but they do not give a clear image. Frosted glass is an example of a translucent material.

Opaque materials do not allow light to pass through. They either absorb or reflect the light and so cast a strong shadow on the side opposite the light. Most everyday objects – including our bodies – are opaque.

This stained glass window has some clear glass, which is transparent, but most of the glass is translucent. The leading between the pieces of glass is opaque.

SEEING THROUGH OBJECTS

Classifying objects as transparent, translucent or opaque.

1. Lay the sheet of white paper on a table.

2. Using the books as props, set up the raybox so that it points downwards at the paper. It should be about 30 cm from the paper. Switch on the raybox and darken the room.

3. Hold the material you are testing upright between the raybox and the paper.

MATERIALS

- a raybox and card with one slit
- some books
- a large sheet of white paper
- small sheets of the following: clear glass, cellophane, frosted glass, paper tissue, waxed paper, thick paper, thin paper, thin silk, heavy cloth, wood, kitchen foil

4. Shine your raybox beam on to each of the materials in turn. Classify the materials as transparent, translucent or opaque.

5. Record your results in a chart like the one at the bottom of the page. In column 2 insert 'most', 'some', 'a little', or 'none'. In column 3 insert 'transparent', 'translucent' or 'opaque' as appropriate.

6. List all the materials in order, with the most transparent at the top of the list, and the most opaque at the bottom.

Is your test of comparison between the different materials a fair test? If not, explain why. Are clouds in the sky transparent, translucent, or opaque? Explain your answer.

Did you know?

The glass or plastic lenses of sunglasses work by letting only some light through while the rest is absorbed or scattered by the lenses. This allows the wearer to see clearly but reduces the amount of light entering the eyes.

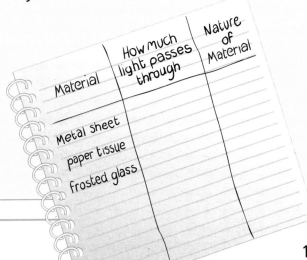

Material	How much light passes through	Nature of Material
Metal sheet		
paper tissue		
frosted glass		

ME AND MY SHADOW

A shadow forms when light from one direction strikes an opaque object. The light, unable to pass through the object, is stopped, and because light travels in straight lines, a shadow is cast on the far side of the object away from the light. The shadow forms an outline of the object.

Some shadows cast a sharp outline. Others have a less clear outline and have two parts – a dark inner region called the umbra and a lighter outer region called the penumbra. The penumbra receives some scattered light which makes the edge of the shadow blurred.

INVESTIGATING SHADOWS

1. Hold the sheet upright. Then place the slide projector about 2 m away from the sheet and pointing at it.

2. Switch on the projector and darken the room.

3. Stand two of your friends of similar height and size between the light source and the sheet. One should be close to the sheet and to one side of the beam. The other should be further away and to the other side.

MATERIALS
- a large white sheet
- a slide projector
- a table lamp with a shade

4. Move round to the far side of the sheet and look at the shadows cast by your two friends. Whose shadow is bigger? What happens to the sizes of the shadows when your friends change positions? Experiment to find out what determines the size of the shadow.

5. Now repeat what you did before, but using the table lamp in place of the projector. Do these shadows have sharper or more blurred edges than before? What makes a shadow have sharp or blurred edges?

A SHADOW PLAY

1. Decide on a story you would like to act out using shadow puppets.

2. Cut out the main characters in card, making sure that each has a clear outline. Tape each shape on to a straw.

MATERIALS

- a large white sheet
- a slide projector
- sheets of thin card
- scissors
- sticky tape
- plastic straws

3. Hold up the sheet and then set up the slide projector about 2–3 m from it. Darken the room. By holding up the puppets between the projector and the sheet, you will be able to project a shadow on to the sheet.

4. Practise performing your play.

5. Try various effects such as changing the size of the shadow, making the shadows overlap, and making shadows appear and disappear.

6. Make sure that your own shadows are not cast on the screen.

7. When you are happy with the result, ask your parents or friends to sit on the other side of the sheet as the audience while you perform your play.

HOW WE SEE THINGS

You may think that we see things around us by sending out a beam from our eyes to the object we are seeing. In fact, the reverse is true. We see by reflected light. Light from the Sun, or some artificial source like a light bulb, bounces off the objects we are observing. This light enters our eyes and is detected by two sets of cells at the back of the eye in a layer called the retina. One of these sets of cells – called rods – are the ones we depend on when there is little light available. They do not produce colour vision, but allow us to see in black-and-white and shades of grey. The other set of cells, called cones, detect colour but only operate when plenty of light is available. Rods and cones get their names from their shapes – cone cells are wider than rods.

This simple experiment will show how we see by reflected light and how the light-sensitive cells in our eyes respond to different amounts of light.

This photograph shows the rods and cones of the eye greatly magnified. The orange coloured cells are the rods. The blue cells are the cones.

SEEING BY REFLECTED LIGHT

MATERIALS

- a shoebox and lid
- a sheet of card
- matt black poster paint
- a paintbrush
- a modelling knife
- a cutting board
- any multi-coloured object

1. Paint the inside surface of the lid and box with black paint. Allow to dry.

2. Carefully cut two slits about 4 cm x 2 cm in the lid of the shoebox, one slit at either end.

3. Place the multi-coloured object at one end of the box and replace the lid. Make sure that no light can enter the box except through the cut-out slits.

WARNING! Take care using the modelling knife and cutting board.

6. Now remove the card and ask your friend to identify the colours of the object by looking through the slit as before.

Can we see an object in complete darkness? Can we see colour in poor light?

4. Place a sheet of card over the slit at the same end as the multi-coloured object. Then get a friend to look into the slit at the other end of the box. Can your friend identify the object?

5. Now move the piece of card slightly and allow a little light to enter. Can your friend identify the object now? Can he or she describe the colours of the object?

> **Did you know?**
> Eating raw carrots may help you see in the dark. Carrots contain vitamin A, a chemical that is used in making a pigment that traps light in the rod and cone cells in the retina.

ON REFLECTION

We have already seen (pages 14-15) that most objects do not produce light of their own. Instead, we see these objects because of the light they reflect. It would be almost impossible for you to read this book in a darkened room. Switch on the light, however, and all is revealed. Light rays from the light bulb are reflected from the book and into your eyes.

The pages of a book reflect light well. Do this experiment to find out how well other things reflect light.

REFLECTIVE POWERS

MATERIALS
- a raybox and card with one slit
- books
- a small flat, or plane, mirror
- two sheets of kitchen foil
- a sheet of black paper
- a sheet of white paper
- a large sheet of grey card
- modelling clay
- a ruler

1. Using the books as props, set up the raybox so that it points downwards at an angle. Switch on the raybox and darken the room.

2. Place a flat mirror face upwards at the point where the beam from the raybox strikes the table.

3. You may be able to see the light beam striking the mirror and bouncing off at an angle. Whether the beam is visible or not, you can intercept it. Using modelling clay, mount the grey card upright so that the reflected light beam strikes the card.

4. Notice the size and brightness of the patch of light formed where the light beam strikes the card. The smaller and brighter the patch of light, the better the reflective power of the material. Use a ruler to measure the size of the light patch. Make a note of the size and brightness of the patch and enter the observation in a chart like the one shown at the bottom of this page.

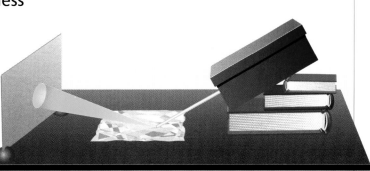

5. Take the two pieces of kitchen foil. Crumple one into a ball and then flatten it out again.

6. Now test the crumpled foil and the smooth foil and all the other materials in the same way as the mirror. In each case, make a note of the size and brightness of the patch of light produced by the reflected light.

7. Work out which surface is best at reflecting light and which is worst. Then place the other three surfaces in order in between.

What makes materials good at reflecting light? What makes them poor at reflecting light?

Material	Size and brightness of light spot
Mirror	
Smooth foil	
Wrinkled foil	
Black paper	
White paper	

MORE REFLECTIONS

You will have noticed in the experiment on pages 16-17 that when the light beam hits a mirror or reflective surface at an angle, it bounces off at another angle. The angle of the incoming beam is called the angle of incidence. The angle of the reflected beam is called the angle of reflection. You can measure the angles of incidence and reflection in this experiment.

MEASURING ANGLES

1. Use the ruler to draw a straight line near one edge of the sheet of card. Measure the half way point and mark it 'O'.

2. Now use the protractor and ruler to draw a second line at exactly 90° to the point that you marked 'O' on the first line you drew. You should end up with a large 'T' drawn on your card.

MATERIALS
- a raybox and card with one slit
- a cork tile
- a sheet of white card the same size as the cork tile
- 10 pins in assorted colours: 4 of one colour and 3 pairs of different colours
- a small plane mirror
- modelling clay
- a ruler and a pencil
- a protractor
- coloured pencils or felt-tip pens

3. Pin the corners of the paper or card to the cork tile using the four pins of the same colour.

4. Use modelling clay to mount the mirror upright exactly on the cross-bar of the 'T', facing the upright.

5. Switch on your raybox and darken the room. Position the raybox to the left of the mirror so that the light beam strikes the mirror at point 'O'.

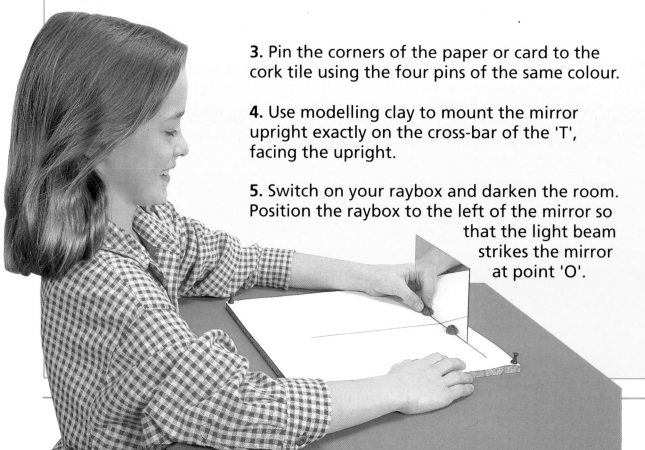

6. Choose two pins of the same colour and use them to carefully mark the path taken by the light beam both before and after it bounces off the mirror.

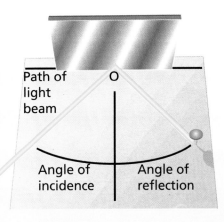

Path of light beam

O

Angle of incidence

Angle of reflection

7. Now change the angle at which the light beam strikes the mirror. Check that the light beam still strikes the mirror exactly at point 'O'. Use two pins of another colour to mark the new positions of the light beam.

8. Repeat what you did before but with the light beam at a new angle.

9. Finally, what happens when you shine the light beam directly at the mirror along the upright of the 'T'?

10. Turn on the light and remove the raybox and mirror. You are left with the 'T' and three pairs of pins. With a ruler draw straight lines in three different colours from each pin to point 'O'. Draw arrows on the lines to show the direction of the original light beams. Label the lines 1, 2 and 3.

11. Remove the pins and with a protractor measure the angle of incidence and the angle of reflection for each light beam. What do you notice about the two angles for each light beam?

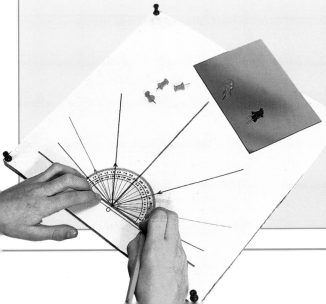

MIRROR, MIRROR ...

A mirror is a superb reflector. Its surface is so smooth and shiny that it reflects light cleanly and gives a clear reflection. The mirrors in our homes are usually made of glass with a silvery coating on the back. Shop or office windows often act like mirrors too, especially those with tinted or reflective glass. But there are also natural mirrors. In still, sunny conditions the surface of a lake may act as a mirror.

A smooth lake gives an almost perfect reflection of this mountain scene.

YOUR MIRROR IMAGE

MATERIALS

● a large plane wall mirror

1. Look at your reflection in a large wall mirror. Where does your reflection appear to be – in front or behind the mirror? Does the reflection appear to be the same distance away from the mirror as you are yourself, or is it nearer or further?

2. Wink your right eye. Which eye winked back at you in your reflection? Raise your left hand. Which hand was raised in your reflection?

3. Is your reflection the right way up and right way round, left to right? Is it the right way up but reversed left to right? Is it upside down and reversed left to right?

If you walk behind a mirror you cannot find your reflection. It is not really where it appears to be. We call this reflection a virtual or unreal image.

MIRROR WRITING

When you see images in a mirror they look the wrong way round. When writing is reflected in a plane mirror, it too becomes reversed.

1. Write some capital letters on a sheet of paper. Hold it up to a mirror. Do any of the letters look the same when they are reversed?

2. Now try to write the letters so that they can be read correctly in a mirror. Check them in the mirror and keep correcting them until you get them right.

Ambulances and other emergency vehicles often have mirror-writing painted on the front. Why is this? Write 'AMBULANCE' as it would appear on the front of the vehicle. How would 'AMBULANCE' be written on the back? Why is this?

Symmetry

When an object can be divided along one or more lines into parts that are exact reflections of one another, the object is said to be symmetrical. Most animals have right and left halves that are mirror images of one another. This is called bilateral symmetry and the animal is bilaterally symmetrical. We are bilaterally symmetrical, although our two halves are not exactly identical as the photo of the boy's face below shows.

Normal face   *Two left halves*   *Two right halves*

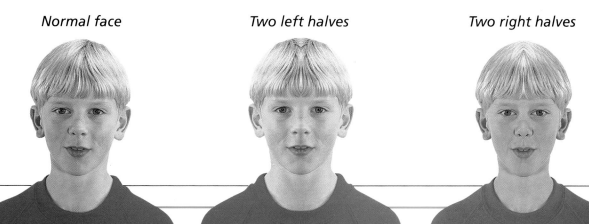

MIRROR IMAGES

Not all mirrors are plane mirrors. Some mirrors bend outwards. These are called convex mirrors. Some bend inwards. These are called concave mirrors.

In this experiment we are going to use a raybox to find out what happens when rays of light are bounced off different kinds of mirror.

SEEING REFLECTED RAYS

1. Mount the plane mirror upright on the large white sheet of paper using the modelling clay.

2. Place the raybox about 60 cm from the mirror and straight on to it. Switch it on and then darken the room. Examine the rays of light reflected from the mirror.

3. Now alter the position of the raybox to shine the five rays at the mirror from a different angle. This test should confirm the result you found in an earlier investigation (see pages 18-19). For a plane mirror, the angle of incidence and the angle of reflection are the same.

MATERIALS

- a raybox with five slits
- a large sheet of white paper
- a smaller sheet of white paper and a pencil
- a plane mirror, a concave mirror and a convex mirror
- modelling clay

---

4. Replace the plane mirror with the concave mirror and set up the raybox about 30 cm directly in front of the mirror.

5. What happens to the light rays when they are reflected from the concave mirror? Make a drawing of what you see.

Concave mirror

Look at this fairground crazy mirror. This mirror makes the children look fatter and shorter. Is it concave or convex? If the mirror made them look long and thin, then would it be concave or convex?

6. Replace the concave mirror with a convex mirror and repeat the set up as for the concave mirror.

7. What happens to the reflected light rays now? Make a drawing of what you see.

Imagine you were looking in a concave mirror and your face was about 15-20 cm in front of it. What would you see? Would your face appear larger or smaller than in real life? Check the answer for yourself by looking into your concave mirror.

If your face were about 15-20 cm in front of the convex mirror what would you see? Would your face appear larger or smaller than in real life? Check the answer for yourself by looking into your convex mirror.

There are many kinds of mirror and they do different jobs. What type of mirror – concave or convex – would be used as a shaving or make up mirror? Why? What kind of mirror would be used as a car driving mirror? Why?

Convex mirror

UP PERISCOPE!

Light travels in straight lines but we can make it go around corners by bouncing it off mirrors.

When light bounces off a flat mirror it leaves the mirror surface at the same angle as it arrived. This property is used in the design of a periscope – a device used for seeing over or around an obstacle.

The periscope allows a person to observe an object from a hidden or protected position. There are many kinds of periscope, but all include a tube with a mirror at either end. In use, the tube is held upright and the top mirror is pointed towards the object to be observed. Light from the object reflects off the top mirror, and then off the bottom mirror and into the eyes of the observer. Some periscopes have lenses that magnify the image and make the object appear larger.

Periscopes are especially useful for military purposes. They enable someone in a submarine, an armoured tank or a dugout trench to see what is going on above without being seen.

MAKING A PERISCOPE

MATERIALS
- an empty long, narrow, cardboard kitchen foil box
- heavy-duty dark sticky tape
- a sheet of card
- a ruler
- a pencil
- a protractor
- a modelling knife
- a cutting board
- two plastic mirrors, about 9 cm x 6 cm

1. Carefully remove the serrated cutting edge of the box. Then use a strip of tape to seal the exposed slit in the box.

2. Draw a right-angled triangle with two sides of length 5 cm on the sheet of card using the protractor.

3. Cut out the triangle shape and use it to draw straight diagonal lines on the opposite sides at either end of the box, as shown here. It is important that the diagonal lines are exactly opposite one another.

4. Using a modelling knife, carefully cut a 1 mm wide slot along each diagonal line. These are the 45° slots into which the mirrors will be mounted.

5. Cut two rectangular holes about 6 cm x 4 cm at the ends of two sides as shown. These are the viewing ports.

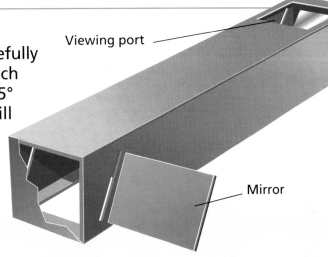

Viewing port

Mirror

6. Now slide a mirror into each diagonal slot so that the mirror surface can be seen through each viewing port.

7. Secure the mirrors by taping them into place and use tape to seal any gaps. This prevents stray light from entering. Your periscope is now complete.

8. Test your periscope by viewing an object from below table level. Is the image you see through the periscope upside down, back to front or the correct way around?

WARNING!

- Take care removing the sharp cutting edge of the box and when using the knife.
- Do not point your periscope at the Sun.

KALEIDOSCOPES

Look into a mirror and you will see one image of yourself. Look in a mirror and hold up another smaller mirror facing the other one, and you will see a never-ending series of mirrors.

By making mirrors face each other you can make multiple images and create marvellous patterns from their reflections. A kaleidoscope is a device that uses several mirrors facing inwards to bounce light off each other. When an object inside the kaleidoscope moves, it produces many reflections in a symmetrical and beautiful pattern.

Two plane mirrors facing each other create an infinite number of images of the apple by reflecting alternate sides of the apple.

MATERIALS

- a piece of card about 25 cm x 15 cm
- a glue-stick
- a ruler
- a pencil
- a metal straight edge
- a modelling knife
- a cutting board
- a sheet of reflective silver plastic wrapping
- a paper tissue or soft cloth
- dark sticky tape
- a transparent or translucent sandwich box lid
- two short strips of wood at least 1.5 cm thick
- tiny pieces of coloured paper or other small colourful objects

MAKING A KALEIDOSCOPE

1. With a pencil, mark off the card along its 15 cm length into three panels each 5 cm wide.

2. Score along the lines with the modelling knife, taking care not to cut right through the card.

3. On the unscored side glue the sheet of silver wrapping, shiny side up. Smooth the foil flat with a piece of tissue or soft cloth.

4. Now fold the card into a triangular tube shape with the mirror surface on the inside.

5. Join the edges of the card together with dark sticky tape. Make sure there is a complete seal along the join so that no light enters.

6. Set the sandwich box lid on the two strips of wood next to a window. Then sprinkle on the tiny pieces of coloured paper.

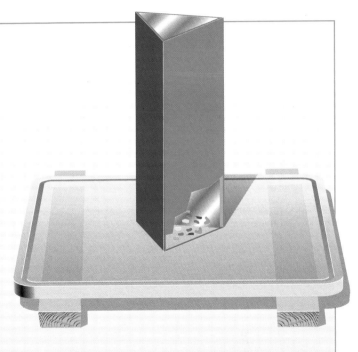

7. Place the tube on top of the bits of paper on the sandwich box lid. Look through the tube and see the patterns produced by the reflections inside the tube. How many sides do the patterns have?

8. Tap the sandwich box lid or turn the tube to change the pattern and colour combinations.

9. Experiment with other small objects, like crystals or small beads.

WARNING!
- Take care using the knife.

Did you know?

The image you see inside a kaleidoscope is an example of radial symmetry. With this type of symmetry, matching parts are arranged around a central point or axis. Some animals and plants show radial symmetry – a sea urchin, for example, and the petals of a daisy or rose flower.

BENDING LIGHT

Have you ever jumped into a swimming pool and then found that the water was deeper than you thought it looked? This effect is caused by the bending of light rays when they travel from one transparent substance to another. This bending is called refraction.

How does this bending of light come about? Light travels fast in air, but more slowly in water, glass and other transparent liquids and solids. However, its speed is still very high; in water, for example, it travels at approximately 225,000,000 m a second.

Water slows light rays in much the same way that it slows down your legs when you walk through a swimming pool. Water is much denser than air. Transparent plastic is denser still.

So light travels fastest in air, slower in water, and slower still through plastic. This slowing of light does not have a noticeable effect when it passes at right angles through the boundary between one substance to another. But when light is hitting the boundary at an angle, then the light is bent.

Did you know?

A mirage is a false view of the sky that looks like a pool of water on the ground. It is caused by a layer of hot air close to the ground refracting light rays from the sky. You can sometimes see mirages above roads on hot days.

This fisherman must aim his spear at a different point from where the fish appears to be to allow for refraction.

BENDING LIGHT THROUGH WATER AND PLASTIC

1. Place a few drops of milk in the water to make it turn slightly murky.

2. Using the box and books as props arrange the raybox so that it is pointing downwards at an angle to the water. Darken the room and switch on the raybox. What happens to the beam of light where it strikes the water surface? If you cannot see the light before it enters the water, hold a glowing joss stick below the beam.

3. Now move the light source so that the beam of light enters at an angle through the side of the container. What happens to the light beam where it strikes the plastic and then enters the water?

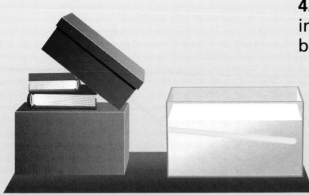

4. In the first part of this investigation you made a light beam travel from air straight into water. In the second part, you made the light beam travel from air, through plastic, and then into water. Was light bent in the same direction and by the same amount in each case? If not, can you explain why?

BENDING MORE LIGHT

Light is bent, or refracted, when it passes from one transparent medium to another. The amount of refraction is related to the density of the substance. Those that are denser slow the light more and cause more refraction. Substances that are less dense, slow light less and cause less refraction.

BENDING LIGHT THROUGH LIQUIDS

1. Fill three of the containers to two-thirds full with the following: one with water to which a few drops of milk have been added; the second with a strong salt solution to which a few drops of food colouring have been added; the third with corn oil. Leave the fourth empty.

2. Using the books and protractor, fix the raybox so that it points downwards at an angle of 45°.

WARNING!
● Take care using the joss stick and matches.

MATERIALS
● a raybox and card with one slit
● boxes and books as props
● a protractor
● four transparent square or rectangular straight-sided containers
● two teaspoons
● a joss stick and a box of safety matches
● corn oil
● food colouring
● milk
● water
● salt
● a notebook and a pencil

3. Darken the room and shine the light beam into the container of milky water. Ensure that the beam shines directly into the liquid and not through the side of the container. If you have difficulty seeing the beam of light before it enters the water, hold a glowing joss stick below the beam.

4. Measure the angle by which the light is bent at the boundary between air and water. Record your result.

5. Repeat the test with the salted water and then with the oil, recording your results as you go.

6. Which liquid bent the light the most? Which bent the light the least? What does this tell you about the densities of the three liquids? Which is the most dense and which is the least dense?

7. For a spectacular finish, carefully pour all three liquids into the fourth container like this: Fill the fourth container one-third full with the most dense liquid. Now very gently pour the next most dense liquid on to the back of a spoon held just above the first liquid. You should be left with two separate layers, one floating on the other.

8. Repeat this using the other spoon and the least dense liquid, so that this forms a third layer floating on top of the other two.

9. Shine your angled beam of light down into the container and you will see a spectacular sight!

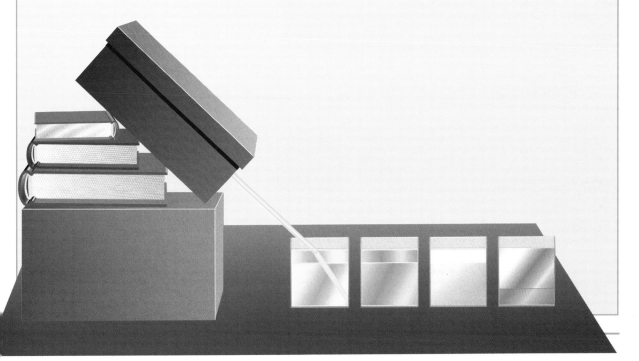

TAKING A SNAPSHOT

If you have ever looked inside a camera you will have seen that it is a light-proof box with a small hole covered by a lens on one side and photographic film on the other. The film records an image as seen through the lens.

The first cameras were based on a device called the camera obscura (Latin for 'dark chamber'). This was a light-proof room with a small hole in one wall. Light from outside shone through the hole forming an upside-down image of the view outside. This was projected on to the inner wall opposite the hole.

The Italian inventor Leonardo da Vinci (1452-1519) was one of the first to describe how the camera obscura worked.

A series of high-speed photographs of pole vaulter David Tork in action.

A simple camera obscura

The term camera obscura refers to an enclosed dark room or box into which light passes through a small hole or lens to produce an image on ground glass or paper. The problem with the camera obscura, invented in Italy in the sixteenth century, was that the image could not be recorded.

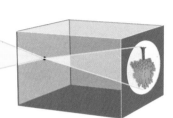

MAKING A PINHOLE CAMERA

1. Use the hammer and nail to punch a hole in the centre of the base of the tin. Cover this hole with two strips of tape.

2. Use a pin to pierce a small hole in the tape through the centre of the hole in the tin.

3. Wrap the circle of waxed paper tightly over the open end of the tin and secure it in place with the rubber band. Ensure that the paper makes a flat surface. The paper is the viewing screen.

4. Stand 4-5 m away from a bright window. Drape the dark cloth over your head and over the camera's viewing screen.

5. Hold the camera at arm's length and point the pinhole at the window. Look at the viewing screen. What do you see? Is the picture upside-down or the right way up? Is the picture dim or bright? Is it larger or smaller than the window? Is the picture clear or blurred?

6. Now take the pin and pierce four new holes around the original pinhole. What do you see on the viewing screen now?

7. Use the nail to enlarge the original pinhole so that it is the same size as the nail hole in the tin. Now what do you see on the viewing screen?

MATERIALS

- a medium sized empty tin
- a dark cloth, 1 m x 1 m
- a pin
- a hammer and a large nail
- scissors
- heavy duty dark sticky tape
- a circle of waxed paper slightly larger than the base of the tin
- a rubber band

WARNING!

- Take care when using the hammer and nails.
- Do not point your pinhole camera at the Sun.

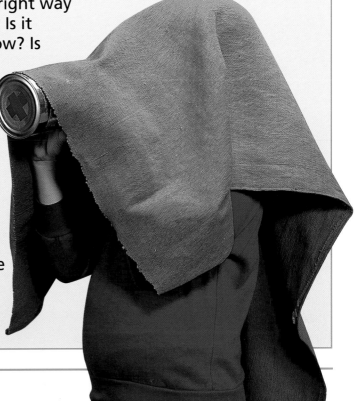

LENSES

We have seen (pages 28-31) how a ray of light passing through flat transparent plastic or glass is bent, or refracted. A lens is a piece of transparent glass or plastic with a curved surface. Convex lenses bend outward and concave lenses bend inwards.

In the experiment below you will find out what happens to light when it passes through convex and concave lenses.

LIGHT THROUGH A LENS

1. First fix the convex lens upright on the white card using the modelling clay.

2. Then set the raybox so that it faces the lens, about 15 cm away from it.

3. Turn on the raybox and darken the room. What happens to the rays of light when they pass through the convex lens? Draw the path of the light before and after it passes through the lens.

4. Now repeat the experiment with the concave lens. What happens to the rays of light this time? Draw the path of the light before and after it passes through the lens.

MATERIALS

- a raybox with five slits
- a rectangular convex lens and a rectangular concave lens
- a piece of white card
- paper and a pencil
- modelling clay

There is a lens near the front of your eye. When you look at an object, light rays from the object are refracted by the transparent front of the eye – the cornea – and by the lens of the eye. The light rays are focused to form an image on the retina at the back of the eye. The image on the retina is upside down and back to front. This information is sent along the optic nerve to the brain. The brain then 'turns' the image the right way up.

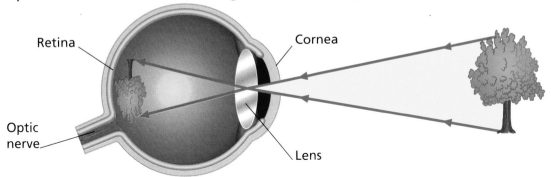

Retina

Cornea

Optic nerve

Lens

HOW WE SEE

1. Point the magnifying glass at a brightly lit window and hold a sheet of paper upright a short distance behind the magnifying glass lens.

2. Move the paper towards and away from the magnifying glass until a clear image of the window appears on the paper.

3. Is the image of the window larger or smaller than the window itself? Is the image upside down or the right way up? The magnifying glass represents the lens of the eye. What part of the eye does the paper represent?

MATERIALS
- a magnifying glass
- a sheet of plain paper

WARNING!
- Do not look at the Sun directly or point your magnifying glass at the Sun.

IN FOCUS

The lens in the eye is able to change shape so that near or far objects can be precisely focused on the retina. When you look at a near object, the lens bulges and bends the light rays more in order to focus the near object on the retina. When you look at a more distant object, the lens narrows, the light rays are bent less, and the distant object is focused on the retina.

Some people have eyes that do not focus properly, so they wear glasses or contact lenses. People who are short-sighted can see well close up but are unable to focus on objects a long way off. Such people have eyeballs that are too long, or lenses of the eye that are too thick. This causes the light to be refracted too much when it enters the eye. When they look at a distant object the image is focused in front of the retina so that the image on the retina is blurred.

Short sight

For distant viewing, point of clear focus is in front of retina

Long sight

For close viewing, point of clear focus is behind retina

People who are long-sighted can see distant objects well but are unable to focus on near objects. They either have eyeballs that are too short, or lenses of the eye that are too thin. When looking at a near object, the light entering the eye is not refracted enough. The image is focused behind the retina and as a result is blurred.

This investigation will show which types of lens are needed to correct long-sighted and short-sighted vision.

CORRECTING EYE PROBLEMS

MATERIALS

- a small magnifying glass
- a desk lamp
- a biconvex lens and a biconcave lens
- a sheet of plain white card
- modelling clay

1. Make two supports for the card out of modelling clay. These should hold it upright, but allow you to move it backwards and forwards.

2. Hold the magnifying glass between the lamp and the card about 1 m away from the lamp. Switch on the lamp.

3. Move the card towards and away from the magnifying glass until a clear image of the lamp appears on the card.

4. Now move the paper backwards away from the lamp so that the image of the lamp is slightly out of focus. This represents the situation for a short-sighted person – the image is being focused in front of the card (or the retina).

5. Experiment by placing first the convex lens and then the concave lens just in front of the magnifying lens. Which lens sharpens the image on the card?

6. With the magnifying glass in position move the paper forwards so that the image of the lamp is once more in focus. Now move the paper forwards towards the lamp a bit more so that the image is slightly out of focus. This represents the situation for a long-sighted person – the image is being focused behind the card (or the retina).

7. Experiment again by placing first the convex lens and then the concave lens just in front of the magnifying lens. Which lens sharpens the image on the card?

8. Which type of lens – convex or concave – is used in spectacles to correct short-sighted vision? Which type of lens is used to correct long-sighted vision?

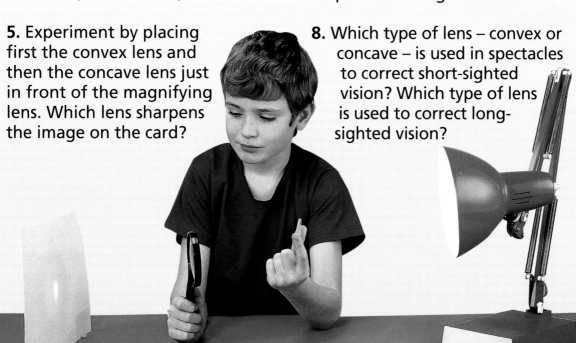

SEEING DOUBLE

Our eyes are set on the front of the head facing forwards. Having two eyes on the front of our head helps us to judge distances. Many animals that hunt for their food have eyes in the front of their heads, too. This enables them to judge how far away their prey is when they are stalking and chasing. On the other hand, the animals that they are hunting often have their eyes set on each side of their head. This enables them to see all around them and spot any would-be predator.

Each of our eyes sees a slightly different view of the same object. This gives our vision 'depth' – we see things in three dimensions (3D). It is easy to show this by simple investigation.

An owls needs both eyes at the front of its head so that it can judge distances accurately when hunting.

TWO VIEWS OF THE WORLD

1. Extend your right arm and hold up your thumb. Close your left eye and look at your thumb with your right eye.

2. Line up your thumb with a distant object – a tree or a church spire, for example.

3. Without moving your thumb, close your right eye, open your left and look at your thumb. Which way has your thumb appeared to move?

4. Still keeping your thumb still, close your left eye, open your right and look at your thumb. Which way has your thumb moved now?

FIELD OF VISION

The area we see with each eye is called the field of vision. The fields of vision of our two eyes overlap. See this for yourself.

1. Hold your head still and close your left eye. Look straight ahead with your right eye.

2. Now extend your right arm out to your side at a height level with your shoulder. Hold up your thumb.

3. Keeping your arm straight, gradually move your arm forwards. Notice the point at which your thumb comes into view.

4. Keep your head still, with your left eye closed and your right eye looking straight ahead.

5. Extend your left arm out to your side and level with your shoulder. Hold up your thumb, and slowly swing your left arm forwards. Notice the point at which your left thumb comes into view. For your right eye, is the field of view wider on your left or on your right?

6. Repeat the above but with your left eye open and your right eye closed. For your left eye, is the field of view wider on your left or on your right?

Overlapping views

If you could plot the field of view of your two eyes it would look something like the picture here. There is an area in the centre of your field of vision that both eyes can see. This is your overlapping field of vision. What stops the fields of vision of your two eyes overlapping more?

Area seen by left eye

Area seen by both eyes

Area seen by right eye

39

MAKING RAINBOWS

The light we receive from the Sun we call white light. However, it is not simply white. It is composed of six main colours: red, orange, yellow, green, blue and violet. This sequence is called the colour spectrum. We see these colours when sunlight shines through raindrops and creates rainbows. The raindrops refract white light and cause the separation of colours. Each colour is refracted by a slightly different amount as it passes into and then out of a raindrop. Red light is bent the least and violet light the most.

We can create a spectrum by refracting sunlight through water.

MATERIALS

- a glass tumbler of water
- a large sheet of white paper
- a cardboard box

MAKING A RAINBOW

1. Choose a clear morning at a time when the Sun is fairly low in the sky.

2. Place a tumbler of water on a box about 4 m away from a window that is receiving direct sunlight. You should be able to see the rainbow spread of colours on the floor as the sunlight is refracted through the tumbler of water.

3. Place the sheet of white paper where the rainbow falls and try to identify the colours in the rainbow.

Did you know?

Sir Isaac Newton was one of the first people to reason that white light was made up of many colours. He used a glass prism to split white light into its separate colours. Alongside the six main colours attributed to the spectrum today, however, Newton distinguished a seventh colour, indigo, since he believed the number seven had mystical significance.

Rainbows are produced when sunlight is refracted through tiny drops of rain.

TURNING COLOURS WHITE

You can change the rainbow colours back into white.

MATERIALS
- a piece of card about 20 cm x 20 cm
- a pair of compasses
- scissors
- a protractor
- a ruler
- two sharp pencils, one short, one long
- coloured pencils

1. On the card use the compasses to draw a circle 15 cm across. Cut out the circle with scissors.

2. Use the protractor and a pencil and ruler to divide the circle into six equal sections (each is a slice at an angle of 60°). Colour the sections in the order red, orange, yellow, green, blue and violet.

3. Push a short pencil, point first, through the hole in the centre of the circle.

4. Spin the circle like the top and watch the colours appear to merge to white or off-white. When the card slows the colours reappear.

5. When the top is spinning fast our eyes cannot separate out the different colours. They merge and are 'seen' by the brain as white.

SUBTRACTING COLOURS

When light reaches an object, some light is reflected and some is absorbed. However, the object will usually reflect and absorb light of different colours by differing amounts. This is what gives the object its colour. In daylight, most objects we see around us are coloured by the light they reflect, not the light they produce.

When sunlight falls on a sandy beach, for example, the sand absorbs all the different colours in the light except yellow. It reflects the yellow light into our eyes, so the sand appears yellow. White objects look white in sunlight because they reflect all colours equally and absorb very little. Black objects appear black because they absorb almost all the light they receive and they reflect very little.

Although white light is really made up of the six colours of the colour spectrum, it is easier to think of white light as made up of three main colours – red, green and blue. These are the primary colours of light. All other colours (except black) can be made by mixing these colours in different amounts.

The colour of this caterpillar's skin warns predators that it is poisonous.

Filters are made from transparent coloured material. A red filter allows only red light to shine through, a blue only blue light, and so on. Each filter blocks out all other parts of the colour spectrum. Filters are used to create special effects in stage shows such as rock concerts. You may have noticed how coloured spotlights make performers' clothes appear to change colour in strange ways. There are simple rules that govern these colour changes.

The colour of this male oak beauty moth helps it to blend in with its surroundings.

USING FILTERS

MATERIALS

- a torch
- red, green and blue filters or cellophane
- sticky tape
- objects of various colours: white, red, green, blue, yellow, orange

1. Do the investigation in natural light or under ordinary room lighting. Tape the red filter or cellophane over the lens of the torch.

2. Switch on the torch and shine the resulting red beam at objects of various colours from a distance of about 1 m. In each case make a note of the colour the object appears to be when viewed by red light. Enter your results in a chart like the one below.

3. Repeat the investigation using a green filter in place of the red and again using the blue filter.

4. What happens when you shine a coloured beam on to a white surface? What happens when you shine it on to a different primary colour? What do you see if you shine it on to a non-primary colour such as yellow or orange?

ADDING COLOURS

Filters block out some of the light that passes through them. Blue filters block out all the other colours of light except blue. If a blue filter is placed over a spotlight it creates a beam of light the same colour as the filter. But what happens when different coloured beams of light are mixed together?

As we saw on pages 42-43, the three primary colours of light are red, green and blue. Colour television works by mixing together these three colours to create all the other colours. The picture on the screen is made up of tiny dots or stripes of red, green and blue. The combination of illuminated dots or stripes gives the colour of that part of the screen. When you view the screen from a distance, the coloured dots or stripes merge to create a natural-looking picture.

MIXING COLOURS

MATERIALS

- three torches
- red, green and blue filters or cellophane
- sticky tape
- a white wall or large sheet of white card

1. Cover the lenses of three torches with the different coloured filters or cellophane.

2. Check that the three beams of light – one red, one green, one blue – are of roughly equal brightness. If not, add further layers of cellophane until all three are of equal brightness.

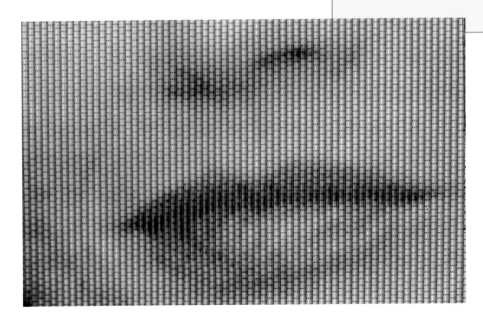

A close up of a television screen reveals the red, green and blue dots that together make up all the colours you see. Any single point on the screen is made up of varying proportions of these three colours.

4. What is the colour of the region where the red and green beams overlap? Describe the colour of the region where the blue and red beams overlap. The proper name for this colour is magenta. Describe the colour of the region where blue and green beams overlap. The proper name for this colour is cyan.

5. What colour would you expect the central area – where all three beams overlap – to be? Is it this colour? If not, can you explain why?

3. Now darken the room. Shine all three torches at a white wall or white card, so that all three beams overlap in a neat arrangement.

Mixing coloured lights is not the same as mixing coloured inks or paints. With printing inks and paints, the primary colours are cyan, magenta and yellow. Compare these colours with those you discovered by overlapping red, green and blue torch beams. What do you notice? The many colours printed on the white paper of this book are made by mixing together the three primary colours of printing inks. On the printed page, combining different amounts of the three primary colours (plus black) produces all the other colours you see.

Cyan

Magenta

Yellow

GLOSSARY

Colour The way our eyes perceive the different components of white light. The range of colours forms the light spectrum: red, orange, yellow, green, blue and violet.

Concave Curving inward as in the bowl of a spoon. The shape of certain lenses and mirrors.

Convex Curving outward as in the back of a spoon The shape of certain lenses and mirrors.

Cornea The transparent outer layer at the front of the eye. It bends (refracts) light slightly.

Focus The point at which light rays meet after they have been reflected or refracted. An image looks sharp when it is in focus.

Image When light rays are bounced (reflected) off a mirror, or bent (refracted) through a lens, they form a copy of an object. This copy is called an image.

Kaleidoscope A device that uses several mirrors all facing inwards. The many reflections inside form attractive symmetrical patterns.

Lens A curved piece of glass or other transparent material that forms an image by bending (refracting) light rays.

Light A special form of energy that can be seen by our eyes. (It is also called visible electromagnetic radiation.)

Opaque Used to describe a substance that does not allow light to pass through.

Periscope A device that reflects light through two right angles and so enables a person to see over or around obstacles.

Pigment A substance that gives colour to the cells and tissues of plants and animals.

Primary colour A pure colour that cannot be made by mixing other colours. All non-primary colours can be made by mixing together the three primary colours in different proportions.

Prism A triangular piece of glass or other transparent material used to split white light into the colour spectrum.

Ray The straight path followed by light as it travels from its source.

Reflection Light rays bouncing off a surface. It is also the name of the image of an object seen in a mirror.

Refraction Light rays being bent as they pass from one transparent material to another.

Retina The light-sensitive layer at the back of the eye. The image is formed on this after light has passed through the lens.

Shadow A dark region that forms beyond an opaque object where it blocks out light.

Spectrum The range of colours that make up white light. The spectrum can be produced by bending (refracting) white light through a prism.

Symmetrical The term for an object that can be divided along one or more lines into parts that are exact mirror reflections of one another.

Translucent Used to describe a substance that allows some light to pass through. Objects cannot be seen clearly through such substances.

Transparent Used to describe a substance that allows all or nearly all light to pass through. Objects can be seen clearly through such substances.

FURTHER INFORMATION

BOOKS

Light Terry Jennings
(Belitha Press, 1995)

Light and Illusion, Action Pack
(Dorling Kindersley, 1995)

Light and Lasers Robin Kerrod
(Oxford University Press, 1993)

*Magic Wand and Other Interactive Experiments
in Light and Colour* Exploratorium Science
Snackbook (Wiley, 1995)

CD – ROMS

Exploring Science – Light and Sound
(Wayland Multimedia, 1997)

ANSWERS TO QUESTIONS

Answers to questions posed in the projects.

Pages 6-7 The inside of the raybox was painted black to prevent light rays being reflected off the box walls, so producing scattered beams of light rather than the narrow beams required.

Pages 8-9 When you move the second card the spot of light disappears from the white card and falls on the second card. This tells you that a ray of light does not bend. It travels in a straight line. When you blow smoke into a beam of light you can see it travelling in a straight line.

Pages 10-11 This is not a fair test because the sheets of materials may not all be of the same thickness. Also they may not be held exactly the same distance from the raybox each time. Clouds in the sky are translucent. They allow some light through but you cannot see through them.

Pages 12-13 The shadow of the friend nearest the projector is bigger. When your friends change position, their shadows change in size. The smaller becomes larger, and vice versa. When using the table lamp in place of the projector, the shadow edges are more blurred. The brighter the lighting, the sharper the edges of the shadows, and vice versa.

Pages 14-15 With the unaided eye, we cannot see objects in complete darkness. We cannot see colour in poor light; we can only see black, white and shades of grey.

Pages 16-17 Materials that are good at reflecting light are smooth, flat and shiny, or light coloured. Materials that are poor at reflecting light are rough, crinkled and dull or dark coloured.

Pages 18-19 When you shine the beam directly at the mirror along the upright of the 'T', the light beam is directed back along its line of travel. The angle that the light beam strikes and bounces off the mirror is the same.

Pages 20-21 The capital letters A, H, I, M, O, T, U, V, W, X and Y remain the same when reversed. Emergency vehicles sometimes have mirror-writing on the front so that drivers in cars ahead see the writing reflected the right way round in their mirrors. On the back of the vehicles the writing is the correct way round.

Pages 22-23 When the light rays are reflected from a concave mirror they converge. When they are reflected from a convex mirror they diverge. Your face would appear larger in a concave mirror and smaller in a convex mirror. A concave mirror would

be used as a shaving mirror because it makes a person's face appear larger. A convex mirror would be used as a driving mirror because it gives a wide field of view.

Pages 24-25 The image in a periscope is the correct way round.

Pages 26-27 The pattern has six sides.

Pages 28-29 When the beam strikes the water it is bent downwards. When it strikes the plastic and then the water it will be bent upwards. The light beam is bent more when it enters plastic and then water because plastic is denser than water and bends the light more.

Pages 30-31 Salted water bends light the most and so is the most dense; oil bends the light least and so is the least dense.

Pages 32-33 The picture is upside down and reversed left to right. It is smaller than the window itself and is dim, but clear. The five pinholes in the pinhole camera produce five images of the window. The large hole produces a bright picture of the window but it is blurred.

Pages 34-35 When light rays pass through a convex lens they converge. When they pass though a concave lens they diverge. The image of the window is smaller than the window itself and is upside down. The paper represents the retina of the eye.

Pages 36-37 For a short-sighted person a concave lens will improve vision. For a long-sighted person a convex lens will improve vision.

Pages 38-39 The thumb appears to move first to the right and then to the left. The field of view of the right eye is wider on the right hand side. Your nose stops the field of vision overlapping more.

Pages 42-43 When you shine a coloured beam on to a white surface it appears to be the same colour as the light beam. When you shine the beam on to a primary colour, a non-primary colour is produced; when you shine it on to a non-primary colour the surface takes on the colour of the light beam.

Pages 44-45 The region where the red and green beams overlap is yellow. The central area where all three beams overlap is white. If it is not white it is because one of the coloured beams is brighter than the others. The overall lighting within the room will also affect the central colour.

INDEX